Fruits of Desire:

Poetry

By: Gulfrey Clarke

Published by Cocoon Publishers

co**CoOn**
PUBLISHERS

Bern Switzerland

http://gulfreyc77.wix.com/gulfreyclarke

ISBN: 978-3-9524291-3-6

Dedicated to:

The advancement of global consciousness from the bottom-side up. Their goal is to dumb you down into quietly accepting an early grave without any resistance, trapped by greed-driven enslavers Our goal is spiritual unity which neutralizes oppression with love.

PREFACE

These poems echo my observations and convictions along lean years of heightening disappointment in humanity. Yet their intentions are not to condemn any race, sex, sect, colour, creed or person, but rather is an honest cry for change that could spark constructive evolution within each global citizen; a purging force to restore peace, love and blessings to all. *IMAGINE!* Nurturing a naturally all-encompassing form of spirituality, which rapidly increases fair play by empowering greedless values, as all types of religion and pain decrease. *A GRAND AWAKENING...*For I am but a conveyor of words rhythmically passed down to me in whispered throbs, during many ponderous moments.

Dates on the materials indicate what batch of writings the poem came from and the period in time when the poem was crafted.

Furthermore, I am indeed grateful to all of my varied teachers and spirit guides, who while furthering their journeys, exposed me to sound knowledge and wisdom, despite their differences.

FOR ALL THE WRONG REASONS

An abundantly weak
sweet succulent pink
yet deceptively meek
bearer of spiritual inner peace sublime—
'tis what most unconscionable folks
frantically search for
It's that ape—
mad-man-of-female
being macho sweetie
Savagely assaulting you
at your very core
She's vicious!
He's malicious!
Simultaneously they cried
Both ambitious
pain-ridden
unprincipled creeps!
Destroying membranes
and brain cells
but still you endure

Pretentious male
vital member of mankind

we'd love to adore
What egg-spirit-sperm wasted
Oh, what a bore
He's no male leader
no teacher
no preacher
not even man
Who aimlessly revolves,
not evolves
with no plan in hand
Smashing to smithereens
family and brotherhood dreams
Systematically
economically
spiritually
and mentally lost!
Blue like in blues
Embracing three lives — lies
in pitiful roles posturing
regrettably poor
unmentioned
adulterated
impure

Far too many well-heeled
raging yellow bones
—full moons
Calculating female energies

demanding more, more, more
Mega greenbacks down the drain
for intense psychological pain
More green
non-taxable green
It's just that plain,
if you know what I mean
Take all his green
strip that Dog clean
— he's so insane
More physical pain
for less spiritual gain
Now ain't that a shame?
Yet she'll cream more cream,
than a healthy Great Dane
Can anyone see truth within her?
Or from behind false glitter
find love in the heart of female Cain?
Can one cultivate something
from healthy nothingness
alive in that selfish scene?

Upon reaching the essence
of life's lean existence
Eternal spirit of youth
gallantly searching for truth
be still —
Witness disbanding relationships

predicated on paper money
See sheer thought beget —
selfish spirits of distrust
Plied arrogantly
like savages driven by lust
And for nothing or far less
you must give up your best
give us more
more
more
Then from insecure butts
blossom children
of mass chaos
So, find love
or the lack thereof
—in you
as key to all reason
Then experience love
at its absolute best
when put to the test
For in every season
It's sweeter
than all attainable money...Honey! 1987

D

WHILE SITTING IN THE COLD (Metamorphosis)

I see you
yielding sweet golden tree
so rigidly cute
yet unequivocally priceless
one shy sturdy doll
You see me
one hip worn
weather torn
long wide but tall
wooden brown bench
—alone
rejecting loneliness
positioned upon Capital's green sandy mall
Poised amid life's big and small
birds, squirrels, people and all
scurrying, springing, swinging and singing
immersed in the present forever
harmoniously united in nature's wind piercing call
While sitting in the cold!

> I see you
> to flesh
> experience sheer joy
> in rapid transformation
> You see me
> sparked by your tender words
> weaken

but for a moment
changing ever-so-slightly
to crisp winds recitation
How I do adore your firm maiden spirit
searching in gentle wonderment
exposed and pure
in rapidly receding day light
Your slender out-stretched branches
with wind and cold successfully coping
While heaven witness
two mature beings groping
without eloping
both wrapped up in the moment
quietly thinking and hoping
While sitting in the cold!

Standing and sitting
pain before gain
Each with its own serious message
about life and death
joy and pain
summed-up in brief stories untold
Both watching
questioning
and researching each other
Surely you must know
natural yearnings
could only grow

Watching and listening
patiently connecting
as two lives unfold
While sitting in the cold!

Somewhere deep inside
everyone knows
the sight of great happiness
inner peace glowing through debris
Threatened only by an abundance
of bitter-sweet memory
Your leaves are to me reaching out
as I dare to share
with you dear heart
my life
and at least a part
of what I'm really all about
So, before God and man
you feel while I kneel
Two spirits
sitting, standing, sensing,
and touching each other
moving, nearer —
coming closer together
While sitting in the cold!

Opposites in actions
but united in mind
unequal in background
but united in spirit
dissimilar in sexual gender
but united in the fire of desire
Countless images of peace, peace, peace
—unlimited peace
So many textures and riveting colours
quiet beauty to explore
If only we could close or never close the door—
If only we, both bench and tree
could blend together happily
If only it was not so cold outside
If only we could warm each other
If only we knew each other better
If only we could be so bold
While sitting in the cold!

1987

"METAMORPHOSIS"

Glass Windows In My Mind

Car-ta-ta-ta-thooump! Peeuu!
Sssssssssssssssssssss!
Car-ta-ta-ta-ta-thooump! Peeuu! Peeuu!
Ssssssssss!
Feel this!
Feel it!
Sssssssssssssssssssssssssss!
Feel grand, feel woman, feel man
Feel earth-shaking force attack barren land
Feel omen, feel wind, feel sea
Feel the order of the Grand Master's decree, at hand
Count with me, one, two, three, peeuu! Hold on!
Sssssssssssssssssssssssss!

Car-ta-ta-ta-ta-ta-thooump! Thooump! Thooump! Peeuu!
SSSSSSsssssssssssssssssss!
See patience, see sea water's pounding
It's Mother Nature's mystical wand in action
Artfully carving into great strong limestone rocks
Conjuring beauty in rage while she's working through faith
Peeuu! Peeuu! Peeuu! Sssssssssssssssssssss! Splash!
Against angry currents
dare not man nor land make a winning stand
I'll crush you or refresh you while bathing in sea water see
Let wise decisions provide unlimited good fate
For the foolish, watery grave await
Or for those who carelessly bath
not saved by God's timely hand

Car-ta-ta-ta-ta-thooump, thooump, thooump thooump!
SSSSSSssssssssssssssssssssssssssssssssssssssssssssss!

Within distant beach's crystal-clear seas
near unlimited coconut trees
Mercy I do extend to all beyond Hell's rich tunnelled door
Abundant pleasantry, peaceful fish-filled waters
massaging boundless sandy sun-cleansed tender shore
Where car-ta-ta-ta-thooump, thooump, thooump!
Peeuu! SSSSSSsssssssssssssssssssssssssssssssss!
Raging ocean's frightful roar
won't alter one's mental peace no more
Allowing two love birds leave from such fierce winds
Force brought up from earth's hot-bitter-sweet core
And after sunset make sunlight together
Quietly exploring and adoring each other forever more.
1987

TRAUMA

Clip klop clip klop clip klop cabop
Well!
Klop clip klop clip klop clip debop
See!
Sheer fear arises with morning sun
As!
Beef leaves stable under the gun
Feel!
Pressure of hoofs intense pounding
On!
Odd, shaped debris, concrete and hone
Still!
Few pause from pain's hot prod hounding
While!
Selfish proud steers to market run
Towards!
Free trade and death for everyone
Join!
Or locked in dark steel cage retch be
Scum!
Foodless, too weak to protect your buns
Sissy!
New-born or weaning sickly ones
Cold!
Affluent herd stamps joyfully.

Kip kop kip kop kip kop debop
Now!
Kop kip kop kip kop kip capop
Oh!
Dear God please stop this savage trance
Sick!
Heifer applies a trick with lips
To!
Sophisticated thing that dance
Slick!
As toes scream out at rhythmic hips
Grind!
A false stiff pole in false hole prance
Pale!
When gutless beings, fake romance
Fast!
Like a surgeon's knife contusion
Clipped!
Takes tree, bird's nest and all earned green
Lost!
Behind greed's wall of illusion
Yes!
We milk dry balls and dolls you fiend
Slime!
And diseased herd die in confusion.
1987

THE OFFICIAL NIGGER—

REAL LIVING DEFERRED, TAKE ONE!

The official Nigger
that forked tongue house Nigger
Oh, what a piously simple, sugarless, lollipop
A natural spirit-sperm wasted
Proper sucker,
supposedly cream of the best crop
Spineless, pugnacious, she-wolf
whom mother nature regrets
—and father time
as if through prestidigitation
renders full stop

Official Niggers are muddy
yellow-ringed, raging full moons
Now think universal
See them
irrespective of race
sex
sect
colour
or creed
Always vocal and visible
With that snake-like demeanour
wolfs in sheep clothing
killer attitudes in deeds
But still
still a respectable Nigger
Based on selfish
weak

fearful
child-like
dependency and greed
An animal haunted by the present,
unpleasant past created
A beast
not contented,
with basic human needs
Scum
proclaiming no-care less fear
you care, more fear
What a lonely,
realistic
but ridiculous tune

Inwardly—
sworn to reflect a cold
calculating ray of existence
Absolute
sweet nothingness
alive within
Hello!
I mean
Feeling no godliness
not even real pain
no conscience producing shame
for abusing other living things
Not even one iota of ancestral love or devotion
Towards forefather's lost blood
in struggle and gloom
How completely insane
Ruthlessly untamed!

Caught-up, locked-up, slaves
of that artificial green
That all-consuming plastic game
of obsolescence fast lane

Raging full moon upon you
will gladly, mercilessly, rack-havoc
And if seen only by master
will strangle into eternity
an unofficial being
Be it one's mother, father, sister or brother
for unholy gain: mindless Nigger's everlasting lover
From Master
good-boy, good-girl, good-boy, good-girl, good-boy
Cried Mistress
good-girl, good-boy, good-girl, good-boy, good-girl
Better watch dogs for master
than master for master's own property and being
It makes you look bigger
bigger-nigger, bigger, bigger, bigger
A bigger—Nigger, Nigger!

Flaming Nigger
that official Nigger's now lost
in an untimely race
Such a gruelling game,
O' to be in first place
First in sex
sect
colour
or creed.
To be accepted

as equal bloodthirsty hound
Trilateral commission member
or top cat on tribunal
Classicist rat cheats oneself
—and creates it
An official Nigger's funeral tomb

Educated official Niggers tide
now recedes in disgrace
'tis punished most cruelly
by strong master of doom
Stinking Nigger, stinking Nigger
was the controller's cry
Mingled with Nigger's screams
from painful strapping
Just like a cat
being dismembered at home
Pure catnip placed
in that cat's blood with haste
Simple Nigger, simply forgot its allotted space
Six feet under
tied to a tree
two steps behind in the over-all scheme
All based on money
power
fame
and feared pain in a dream. **1978**

Will You Let Me Be?

After tonight's rare passion and drama
will you let me be?
As due drops embrace dry thirsty leaves
would you release my spirit you've joined forever?
Will you accept both the joy and pain of truth's karma?
Knowing we've created a monumental endeavor
A blissful oneness found in never living together

As dawn's blue shadows stroll across sleepy faces
boldly announcing advancing first light
Will your nurturing warmth willingly set my soul free?
Shall we not forget the ecstasy of eternal spirits' night?
Though happy to have lit a candle in divinity
must we quickly disclaim our love's trinity?

When waters darken as sun sets around us
Shall we with sharpened beaks and claws turn killers?
Will we change growth to pale cheap lust and dust?
Godspeed my loveliness as we in peace are parting
'til one day in light love's coming
We will again embrace. 1989

Being Teacher and So Much More.

In one stance
purple sky
dark red clouds
and great Sun
Without sound
moving swift
they become almost one
—ablaze!

Once in youth
quite bright
a delight
Then at midday
a strong raging sort
gently aged at dusk

Timely firm
yet mild tempered rich
golden Sun did request,
"Reduce please to whispers
animals of dry land
Fighting's not for twilight
your work-day is done"

Peacefully sinking
one mystically fading force
although grieved
smiles to young rebels
—pupils of trite cause

Piously leaving girl and boy fishes
twisting weak with remorse—
 abrasive gifted heirs
to a splendid blue ocean

 Shivers creep in
 from the other side
 as natures lone regret approaches
 and daylights all but lost
 A time when gulls nor fishes
feel quite the match
 for advancing storm clouds
 or deep water's dark potion

 Out of thick clinging mist
 surged forth a message
 pure and clear
 "Always be perceptive, balanced, and practical"
 echoed life's sweltering reservoir's ray
 "And remember you fishes — tomorrow!"
 A final glimmer did convey
 "I'll expect nothing less than your absolute best!"

 An owl calls out
 as many quickening shadows play
 And father time crept slowly
 down horizon of West. 1988

7 P.M. CALVIN

SULTRY NOTHINGNESS

See green oak tree
and then see naught
A rich fleeting image
of life few caught

Blazing fashions
make her hollow
While gift of brain
remains shallow

Quiet beauty
of still mountains
Give the needy
clean water fountains

Back seat driver
I fear the most
With sex and car
they create ghost

Like Queen of Sheba
she does enter
To sell sweet goods
mother nature lent her

For her, big money
or land they fight
None for me, kind sir—
I do not seek such plight

From fierce bigots
take war and gun
And let mad gadfly
sting the sultry one

Dear God let me
at last please be
on bended knee
under the willow tree 1996

OBSOLESCENCE

Zombies stop
Compare and contrast
sick drunkard
home at last
To '80s junkie
attending death mass
And racist vampires
money trees without class
In Island's warm sunlight
always first to bask

Now or never
stop please stop
Unhappy victims
of programmed addiction
Doctors and patients
— with full tranquil glares
Despise the nobodies
Child, use strong conviction
Retire a government slicker
without rhyme or reason
One heartless butt-licker
having swallowed their lies
Oh, dear Mother Dear,
you deserve no cheer
And by siding with the enslaver
millions are now lost
child-rejects without a chance
adrift without remorse

Quit now
if you dare
Colourless genocide inside out
rotting carcasses everywhere
For love eliminates from within
selfish lion share need
Going with the flow
kills babies through greed

Pollution
Prostitution
System's dissolution
In conclusion
Resolution —
Do and be
one energy
who really care. 1988

Into the light of freedom

See yet another spirit-body gasping,
locked in the throes of death's great jaws
Shed not a bitter tear for such a lucky being
patiently travelling, swiftly reaping man's just due
As time presses on for those life adores
stressed out confused shepherd-less sheep,
caught up doing what we all must do
- God's will

A rather tough spot, some might say
witnessing the receding face of one being
humbled with hair, more white than grey
so small yet gentle, tender and fair
—be strong and face the day
I loved you father dear, we quietly mumbled
so be bold with us—
for mother's sake

I hate the stranger you became
dear father dear
If only your truths in deeds
were truths that supported your words
You had answers we never did see
—so, let it be
forthright and true
For it was not about you,
nor me,
just you, in a flash, beating the competition
always the sham artist—for ***the truth's*** sake

simply put, you never trusted me
so be bold with us —
and face the day
be strong for all you have led astray

Now we witness the divine spectacle,
as you're laid out stiffly
with all the pride that one could muster
powerless to protect your deeds, money, or ass
Relentlessly your groupies beg advice
"Room for one more!", shouted the grim reaper
"Coming right up, sir!"
We heard your personal demon reply
Solemn two-faced friends quivered with fright
as foes bowed their heads in remorse

You lost your sons to become boss
used death as excuse to save your ass
Silencing a regrettable ominous past
exposed for all the world to see
Then in one final groan,
up went the ghost at last
"Just remember this you, sniffling fools,
cry only for yourselves
in this fleeting moment of despair
I've gone over and know all now —
Reborn and speechless, wow!
While you know not of future test
or how long be it before your end is
And then like me be laid to rest. 2008

Gulfrey Clarke earned a business degree in the first graduating class of the University of the District of Columbia (WTI) Washington. D.C. 1977, before attending the U. S. D. A. Graduate School of Business.

He withdrew from Howard University to practise accounting and pursue independent research opportunities in American-Caribbean trade policies, relationships, treaties, and MOUs.

In The Bahamas he wrote letters to the editors concerning economic policies and living conditions in 1980.

Gulfrey is a proud husband, father of three and grandfather of two, who finds time for aikido, table tennis, poetry and portrait or landscape oil painting, between English teaching engagements.

He has managed his Steady Steps English School for the past ten years. Using TEFL and CELTA English teaching qualifications from Cambridge University along with a Swiss SVEB 1 add on module; he has taught English in Zurich and Bern Switzerland for 14 years. TELC English Expert/Examiner for past 6 years.

www.ingramcontent.com/pod-product-compliance
Lightning Source LLC
Chambersburg PA
CBHW070050040426
42331CB00034B/2965